THE
FUNNIEST
CHELSEA
QUOTES...
EVER!

About the author

Gordon Law is a freelance journalist and editor who has previously covered football for the *South London Press*, the *Premier League*, *Virgin Media* and a number of English national newspapers and magazines. He has also written several books on the beautiful game.

THE

FUNNIEST

CHELSEA

QUOTES...

EVER!

by Gordon Law

Printed in the United States of America
ISBN-13: 978-1539777991
ISBN-10: 1539777995

Photos courtesy of: Michael Hulf, Ramzi Musallam.

Contents

Introduction

"I'm European champion, I'm not one out of the bottle, I think I'm a special one" was how Jose Mourinho introduced himself to the media when he arrived at Chelsea in 2004.

The manager has since lived up to that now legendary quote by leading Chelsea to three Premier League titles over two spells and treating us to even more priceless quips.

Whether it's using omelettes to describe the quality of his team, coining the phrase "park the bus" or saying young players "...are a little bit like melons", Mourinho's post-match press conferences have always been a hot ticket.

His mind games with Arsenal counterpart Arsene Wenger and rants at referees or any opponent have also been hugely entertaining.

Claudio Ranieri was the original Stamford Bridge quote machine and many of his statements were utterly bonkers. "Football managers are like a parachutist. At times it doesn't open. Here, it is an umbrella. You understand, Mary Poppins." OK, then Claudio...

Dennis Wise's views on football have kept us amused, former chairman Ken Bates was never afraid to speak his mind, while hardman Ron 'Chopper' Harris has his own unique take on playing the game.

Many of their classic lines can be found in this unique collection of quotations and I hope you laugh as much reading this book as I did in compiling it.

Gordon Law

THE FUNNIEST CHELSEA QUOTES... EVER!

PLAYER
POWER

"John Terry – he's a great leader. What can I say about him that I didn't say before? He's a great leader."

Avram Grant

"Maka's normally a one-in-10 man. Most players score nine out of 10 but he misses nine out of 10."

Frank Lampard on Claude Makelele's penalty success rate

"I think [Juan Sebastian] Veron is the best midfielder in the world."

Claudio Ranieri

"A goalkeeper is a goalkeeper because he can't play football."
Ruud Gullit

"Two years ago I watched Carlton play for the reserves and I saw two animals in him – one was a rabbit and the other a lion. I want to see that lion come out in him more often."
Claudio Ranieri on Carlton Cole

"The best Italian this club has signed is the chef."
Frank Leboeuf

"Tommy Docherty and Ron 'Chopper' Harris invented soccer violence. It's when they retired that it spread to the terraces."

Peter Osgood

"Ninety-five per cent of my problems with the English language are the fault of that stupid little midget."

Gianfranco Zola on Dennis Wise

"Watching Ruud was like watching an 18-year-old play in a game for 12-year-olds."

Glenn Hoddle on Ruud Gullit's Chelsea debut

"Mark Hughes is playing better and better, even if he's going great and starting to look like a pigeon."

Gianluca Vialli

"It's been harder this year, Liverpool have got better, Man U have got better, Arsenal have got better, and Tottenham have joined the quartet of five teams."

Joe Cole's maths don't add up

"[Jose] Mourinho is the best coach in the world. He is not God, but he almost is."

Eden Hazard

"The moment I turned up for training and saw [Gianfranco] Zola, I knew it was time to go."
John Spencer

"He is like a shark, like Jimmy Floyd Hasselbaink."
Claudio Ranieri on Adrian Mutu

"I once said Jimmy Floyd Hasselbaink is like a shark and Carlton Cole like a lion. Well, Adrian Mutu is another born predator. In fact, Mutu is like a snake."
Claudio Ranieri

"I made a speech before the game at Middlesbrough in the dressing room and afterwards John Terry said, 'Now you are a man'. If John Terry says I am a man then I am a man."

John Obi Mikel

"The Doc used to tell me, 'Be sure to get your tackles in early'."

Ron 'Chopper' Harris on advice from Tommy Docherty

"Wisey said I think too much. But I have to do all his thinking for him."

Gianfranco Zola on Dennis Wise

"In 'Something About Mary', there's a fella called Ted. He's a pure lookalike from Franco Zola."

Jody Morris

"I try to learn the language, but every time I go some place like Dennis Wise, my English go down."

Gianfranco Zola

"My confidence is 100 per cent in Frank Lampard, but I told him if the next penalty is at a key point, then it's better for another player to take the responsibility."

Jose Mourinho

"When you see Damien [Duff] coming out of the shower, you'd never believe he's a professional footballer."

Didier Drogba

"Luca wears some bad, bad underpants – like my grandfather wore. Big white underpants like they used 40 years ago."

Roberto Di Matteo on Gianluca Vialli

"I like to think that, apart from being a bit of a butcher, I've something else to offer."

Ron 'Chopper' Harris

THE FUNNIEST CHELSEA QUOTES... EVER!

"My fondest memory of him is his passport picture, which was a Panini sticker of himself."
Michael Duberry on Mark Hughes

"Luca [Vialli] thinks he looks like Bruce Willis but I think he looks more like Bruce Forsyth."
Chelsea kitman Aaron Lincoln

"Why am I the best in the world? Because I am, that's all."
Claude Makelele

"If someone needed sorting out, he'd do it."
Jody Morris on Dennis Wise

"I think John Terry's got a hell of a future. The only difference between him and me is that, when I tackled, they didn't get up."
Ron 'Chopper' Harris

"I used to share a room with Gianfranco Zola but I had to throw him out because he snored so much."
Robert Di Matteo

"The English players speak fast and they talk with an accent. When I'm walking around the streets of London, people speak so fast that I don't know what they are saying."
Michael Ballack

"When the first foreign players came to Chelsea there was a book of Cockney rhyming slang going round. One day in a team meeting Ruud [Gullit] suddenly said, 'I'm a grave digger and a very rich one'."

Dennis Wise

"Have you seen the size of Jimmy Floyd Hasselbaink's hooter? It's the biggest in the club. But cop a look at John Terry's, because it's not that far behind. It's a beaut."

Jody Morris

"He is my new little lion. And I like lions."

Claudio Ranieri on Hernan Crespo

"They call me 'The Radio' because I talk. I love talking. I can't help it. It's a family problem. My wife speaks a lot. My father's always talking. Sometimes at home we need to do a time-out, like in basketball, to stop everybody from talking."

Gus Poyet

"Every time I see him [Mikael Forssell] it reminds me to buy a pint of milk on the way home."

Aaron Lincoln, Chelsea kitman

"Graeme Le Saux takes a lot of stick from people because he's wise, but it's just the way he is and he's a great geezer."

Frank Lampard

"You don't speak English, mate! Three years here and you don't speak English!"

Cesc Fabregas interrupts an interview to have some banter with teammate Oscar

SAY THAT AGAIN?

"It is omelettes and eggs. No eggs – no omelettes! It depends on the quality of the eggs. In the supermarket you have class one, two or class three eggs and some are more expensive than others and some give you better omelettes. So when the class one eggs are in Waitrose and you cannot go there, you have a problem."

Jose Mourinho referring to lack of transfer funds being available to him

"The moral of the story is not to listen to those who tell you not to play the violin but stick to the tambourine."

Jose Mourinho

Say That Again?

"If it is the case that you need just a first 11 and three or four more players, then why did Christopher Columbus sail to India to discover America?"

Claudio Ranieri explains his tinkering

"The flight of the ball was really amazing. It was far and high and then it just fell low."

Petr Cech gets all scientific

"We must have had 99 per cent of the game. It was the other three per cent that cost us the match."

Ruud Gullit

"I have a number of alternatives and each one gives me something different."
Glenn Hoddle

"Sometimes you see beautiful people with no brains. Sometimes you have ugly people who are intelligent, like scientists."
Jose Mourinho on the poor standard of the Stamford Bridge pitch

"Yoghurts are down at Asda."
Graeme Le Saux when asked for his 'save of the month'

Say That Again?

"Football is like a car. You've got five gears, but the trouble with English teams is that they drive in fourth and fifth all the time... When they crash in Europe they say it's bad luck. It isn't – it's bad driving."

Ruud Gullit

"I couldn't tell you what is wrong with my feet but I've just never liked them."

Claudio Pizarro

"It doesn't matter what happened – we got the three points and that's all that counts."

Wayne Bridge

"[The players] showed good stamina and good vitamins."

Claudio Ranieri after a Champions League win over Arsenal

"Maybe the guy drank red wine or beer with breakfast instead of milk."

Jose Mourinho after a Sheffield United fan threw a bottle at Frank Lampard

"On the pitch, when I see green or smell green, I get a little bit crazy. The grass, you know? I get this green mist."

Jimmy Floyd Hasselbaink

Say That Again?

"Young players are a little bit like melons. Only when you open and taste the melon are you 100 per cent sure that the melon is good. Sometimes you have beautiful melons but they don't taste very good and some other melons are a bit ugly and when you open them, the taste is fantastic... One thing is youth football, one thing is professional football. The bridge is a difficult one to cross and they have to play with us and train with us for us to taste the melon."

Jose Mourinho

"When I read a few things, I smell a few coats."

Jose Mourinho

"Football managers are like a parachutist. At times it doesn't open. Here, it is an umbrella. You understand, Mary Poppins."

Claudio Ranieri on arriving at Chelsea in 2000

"Why drive Aston Martin all the time, when I have Ferrari and Porsche as well? That would just be stupid."

Jose Mourinho on rotating Damien Duff, Joe Cole and Arjen Robben

"With hindsight, it's easy to look at it with hindsight."

Glenn Hoddle

Say That Again?

"It is like having a blanket that is too small for the bed. You pull the blanket up to keep your chest warm and your feet stick out. I cannot buy a bigger blanket because the supermarket is closed. But I am content because the blanket is cashmere. It is no ordinary blanket."

Jose Mourinho on Chelsea's injury troubles

"Nothing was different to other games. What was different was we lost."

Avram Grant

"One coach was training a player's hair, and another was training another part of his body."

Claudio Ranieri

"You may as well put a cow in the middle of the pitch, walking. And then stop the game because there was a cow."

Jose Mourinho on Newcastle United's time-wasting tactics

"I'm very passionate about antiques because they are like people."

Emmanuel Petit

"Envy is the biggest tribute that the shadows do to the man."

Jose Mourinho replies to criticism from Graeme Souness and Jamie Carragher

Say That Again?

"Sometimes it is good to score at 43 seconds... and sometimes it is good to last a little longer."
Roberto Di Matteo

"My team is like an orchestra. To play the symphony correctly, I need the boom-boom but also the tweet-tweet. Sometimes the boom and the tweet go well together."
Claudio Ranieri

"I can't say we are the best in England, but I don't think there is a team stronger than us."
Avram Grant

"There are times when I stand up in front of a full-length mirror and act like a contortionist. I twist my neck and I stare at my ass. My fat butt cheeks aren't a particularly edifying spectacle but... over time it's taught me a lesson: my ass is earthquake-proof."

The opening chapter from Carlo Ancelotti's book

"It's a lance that had to be boiled."

John Terry

"It's great to get that duck off my back."

Gary Cahill

REFFING HELL

"Referees aren't looking at what they should be looking at. You need to prioritise. It seems the main issue this season is whether three or four Chelsea players surround referees, or say things they shouldn't say."

Avram Grant is feeling the pressure

"The circumstances are difficult for us with the new football rules that we have to face. It is not possible to have a penalty against Manchester United and it is not possible to have penalties in favour of Chelsea. It is not a conspiracy, it is fact. I speak facts. If not, I need big glasses."

Jose Mourinho

"You can say the linesman's scored. It was a goal coming from the moon or from the Anfield Road stands."

Jose Mourinho on Luis Garcia's 'ghost goal' for Liverpool in the 2005 Champions League semi-final

"In England, the referees either shoot you down with a machine gun or don't blow their whistle at all."

Gianluca Vialli

"If you ask me if I jump with happiness when I know Mr Poll is our referee? No."

Jose Mourinho doesn't rate Graham Poll

"When I saw [Barcelona coach] Frank Rijkaard entering the referee's dressing room I couldn't believe it. When Didier Drogba was sent off [after half-time] I wasn't surprised."

Jose Mourinho after losing to Barcelona

"How do you say 'cheating' in Catalan? Can [Lionel] Messi be suspended for acting? Barcelona is a cultural city with many great theatres and this boy has learned playacting very well."

Jose Mourinho on Messi's antics after Asier Del Horno was sent off

"The referee made three mistakes only. The red card, playing too much time at the end of the first half and the penalty. Apart from that he was good."

Avram Grant

"I do not know if he is a referee or a thief. There are no words to describe the person who was on the pitch there."

Jose Boswinga is not happy with ref Tom Henning Ovrebo's officiating in Chelsea's match against Barcelona

"The referee was poor. Very, very poor. And it reflected in the result. I spoke to him at the end and I was very aggressive. I don't care if he's OK or not. Anyone can have a bad day but this was not a bad day for us: it was a good day for us but a bad day for the referee. Conspiracy theories can lead to bans and people calling us crybabies, so we're not saying that. But it keeps happening."

Andre Villas-Boas after Chelsea lost to QPR, where referee Chris Foy sent off both Jose Bosingwa and Didier Drogba

"A top referee is an official who treats a player like a man."

Ron 'Chopper' Harris

"People want a storm but there isn't one.
I respect Sir Alex a lot because he's a great
manager, but he must follow the procedure.
I don't speak with referees and I don't want
other managers doing it, it's the rule. One thing
is to speak, one thing is to shout."

Jose Mourinho on Sir Alex Ferguson

"I know the referee did not walk to the dressing
rooms alone at half-time. He should only have
had his two assistants and the fourth official
with him but there was also someone else."

**Jose Mourinho was unhappy Sir Alex
Ferguson spoke to referee Neale Barry as
the teams left the field at half-time**

"Look at the blond boy in midfield, Robbie Savage, who commits 20 fouls during the game and never gets a booking. We came here to play football and it was not a football game, it was a fight and we fought and I think we fought fantastically."

Jose Mourinho

GAME FOR A LAUGH

"Every time I got the ball I looked up and their goal seemed really far away, like it was on the M25."

Didier Drogba

"I didn't get that worked up in the dressing room. Instead, I used to read the programme to see who I had to kick that week."

Ron 'Chopper' Harris

"It doesn't matter what happened in the game – we got the three points."

Wayne Bridge doesn't understand how the Carling Cup final works

"You alwight mate, innit, innit? Speaking Cockney is so funny, especially when you first come over. The first time you hear it you think, 'What is that?'"

Mario Melchiot

"During the actual games, it is as though everybody's brains are switched off."

Florent Malouda

"I can play football at my level for £500 a month because I love it so much."

Marcel Desailly

"Sometimes I dive, sometimes I stand. But I don't care about this. In football you can't stay up all the time."

Didier Drogba

"It's a top club but it's not a top, top, top, club."

Jimmy Floyd Hasselbaink on Chelsea

"Sat in the stand, you're powerless to do anything. You've got fleas in your pants."

Florent Malouda on being left out of the France squad

"The worst crowd trouble I saw was down at Millwall. In the warm-up, there were people coming out of the crowd with meat-hooks in their heads. I think that's the only time I've been frightened in a game."

Ian Britton looks back on a game at The Den in 1976

"The cup with the big ears is the holy grail to me. It starts the child in me dreaming."

Claude Makelele on the Champions League trophy

"In football, I don't like to lose."

Andriy Shevchenko

"I've never seen so much violence on the pitch as in England. Before certain matches, I'm scared an opponent might harm me."

Frank Leboeuf

"We know we have to score goals, be strong in defence and kill teams in the first half."

William Gallas gets threatening

"My accountant could manage Chelsea to fourth or fifth place."

Gianluca Villa on Chelsea's riches under Roman Abramovich

"Obviously there's a language barrier at Chelsea. The majority of the lads speak Italian, but there's a few who don't."

Dennis Wise

"It was obvious from the moment we arrived in Baghdad and saw soldiers carrying machine guns that leisure activities would be limited."

Colin Pates on a club tour to Iraq in 1986

"It's time for a big party with the cup with the big ears."

Roberto Di Matteo after leading Chelsea to Champions League glory

"Chelsea went from being a superpower to a dreadful Second Division side more famous for its hooligan element than its team. The whole place became a rancid meat pie crawling with maggots."

Alan Hudson

"I always spray perfume on my shirt before we play. The other guys are happy with it because they know I smell good when we celebrate. And also when we change shirts after matches, mine smells good even when it needs to be washed."

Florent Malouda

"I don't really mind that I'm only remembered as a bloke who went in hard. It's better than not being remembered at all."
Ron 'Chopper' Harris

"When Vinnie Jones and Mick Harford were in the same side, you'd have needed crash helmets to play against them, never mind shin pads."
Tommy Langley

"I can look back and say, 'I've lived' and that's all down to this old funny game."
Gianluca Vialli

"The Chelsea goalposts have become my friends, next to all the fellows who have been my teammates over the years."

Peter Bonetti

LIFESTYLE CHOICE

"Chelsea were a sausage, eggs and chips club before the foreign players arrived. That's what we ate before training and even before matches."

Dennis Wise

"When you're chatting in the dressing room, the last thing you talk about is football."

Hernan Crespo

"Ed de Goey is the worst-dressed man I've ever seen. One pair of jeans, one pair of trainers, one shirt and one haircut."

John Terry

"I read this piece by the car man, Jeremy Clarkson, saying a footballer goes out in the morning, gets in his Aston Martin, forgets to take a drugs test, takes coke, has a drink, then shags a bird. And that was 'a day in the life of a footballer'. But a lot of players are decent fellas."

Frank Lampard

Q: "What would you have done if you hadn't been a footballer?"

A: "A funeral director. I like looking at dead bodies."

Chris Sutton

"Liverpool won the FA Cup a few years ago with a team of 11 foreigners, including Scots, Welsh and Irish. Now we have Spanish, French and Italians. They speak better English, are more civilised and know how to use a knife and fork."

Ken Bates

"I'll hire a big chauffeur-driven car so I take my kids out for a walk."

Florent Malouda

"I was just as disappointed as Mandela."

Ruud Gullit after his meet with Nelson Mandela was called off

"When I signed for Chelsea, all the papers made out I was an alcoholic and here for the nights out and the booze. But I'm just here to play football."

Damien Duff

"At a French club they buy you champagne and cake on your birthday. Here they shove your face in the mud."

Frank Leboeuf

"I tasted Christmas pudding for the first time this year and it was very good!"

Carlo Ancelotti

Journalist: "Is there any music you like from the Czech Republic?"

Petr Cech: "There's a group named 'Support Lesbians' who are one of my favourite bands."

"I wanted to be a garbage collector. The garbage man would drive past my house with his horse and cart. I loved that. I imagined myself going around the city, driving the cart."

Hernan Crespo

"I don't feel guilty about anything I earn. It's life. Businessmen earn 100,000 times more than us."

Marcel Desailly

"There are magazines, letters, pictures, clothes, creams, everything, he cannot open the door. If he did it would make a bigger day."

Fernando Torres on Juan Mata

"I have a couple of bikes from the [Paris-] Dakar rally. I have a bit of a crazy head and I go into the mountains with the big rocks and almost kill myself. It's my escape."

Andre Villas-Boas

"I read Michael Caine's biography. It was about him growing up."

Frank Lampard

"If you're a playboy and you're not there, you can't win the FA Cup and be second in the Premier League. That's impossible."
Ruud Gullit on why Chelsea fired him as manager

"I get paid on the last Thursday of the month and from there my mam looks after it... I don't go round flashing the cash. That's not me. I came here for ridiculous money. It's not my fault, it's the job I'm in. I didn't ask for the game to be like this. I play because I love the game. That, and the fact that it's the only thing I'm good at."
Damien Duff

"If I'm alone on the road in England, I begin to question whether I'm on the right side of the road. When I go back to Italy, I've started to wonder the same thing."

Claudio Ranieri

"My hair is difficult, it's a problem! It doesn't always look healthy. But there's nothing I can do about it. If it was up to me, I would have chosen a different kind of hair."

Ricardo Carvalho

Q: "Last tin you opened?"

A: "Not tin. Bottle of wine."

Marcel Desailly in the Chelsea programme

"When I first went out for a night with some English players, they couldn't believe I didn't drink. Coke? They said it like they had never heard of such a thing. 'Go on,' they said. 'Have a drink. What's wrong with you?'"

Mario Melchiot

"I've only been to a pub once and that was to get cigarettes for my wife at 11.30 in the evening. I prefer bars to sit and drink tea or coffee."

Jose Mourinho

"I don't have a taste for having 10 cars."

Jose Mourinho

"London is the best city in the world. It's a seaport where hundreds of languages are spoken and where football is played."

Michael Essien knows his facts

"My golf handicap is 16. I'm the only black man who can beat them. They don't want to be beaten by me."

Ruud Gullit

"I played my first rock festival during the summer. I was far more nervous than for any match I've ever played in."

Petr Cech, drummer of the Prague band 'Eddie Stoilow'

"Ooh... It's quite embarrassing actually. I had a little teddy bear called Gordon the Gopher. I took him to bed with me 'cause he was my favourite."

John Terry when asked what his favourite toy was when he was little in a newspaper Q&A

"I advise players to surround themselves with people who don't idolise them. If we commit traffic offences we should pay the fines. And at the restaurant we should wait our turn like others."

Jose Mourinho

"In English, the things you use in casinos are chips, but in Italian we call them fish. So I once said, 'When the fish are down...' Everybody was like, 'What are you talking about?'"
Gianluca Vialli

"If there were a World Drinking XI, Pele would have the No.10 shirt."
Alan Hudson

"I would like to be in a movie. I want to be the bad person who is killed at the end of the movie, like Gary Oldman in Air Force One."
Frank Leboeuf

"If they made a film of my life, I think they should get George Clooney to play me. He's a fantastic actor and my wife thinks he would be ideal."

Jose Mourinho

"I'd like to be Sean Connery, 007 agent."

Gianluca Vialli

"I would love to get to the stage where I can actually write the whole book myself."

Frank Lampard on his children's book: Frankie vs The Pirate Pillagers

BEST OF ENEMIES

"I don't want him to teach me how to lose 4-0 in a Champions League final because I don't want to learn that."
Jose Mourinho after Johan Cruyff was critical of his team's style of play

"Gary Neville say bad, other people say good. When he say this, he don't respect me. The stats show I am up there among the best."
David Luiz on "being controlled by a 10-year-old on a PlayStation"

"Arsenal fans get it I left I won #ihaveastaronmystarnow"
Ashley Cole tweets

"I'm delighted for Claudio Ranieri that we beat Fulham in the FA Cup semi-final, as if we'd lost yesterday, it would have been a pity to sack him just after he'd signed a new contract."

Ken Bates

"I am not concerned about how Chelsea are viewed morally. What does concern me is that we are treated in a different way to other clubs. Some clubs are treated as devils, some are treated as angels. I don't think we are so ugly that we should be seen as the devil and I don't think Arsene Wenger and David Dein are so beautiful that they should be viewed as angels."

Jose Mourinho

"My history as a manager cannot be compared with Frank Rijkaard's history. He has zero trophies and I have a lot of them…"

Jose Mourinho

"If [Rafael Benitez] wants me to stay on my feet, maybe he should tell his defenders to stop hitting me."

Didier Drogba

"[Ken] Bates always had to be one up on you. If you told him you'd been to Tenerife, he'd say he'd been to Elevenerife."

David Speedie

"If I had to choose between the Israelis or Tony Blair to protect me, then Israel wins every time."

Ken Bates not happy some of his players refuse to fly to Israel for a UEFA Cup tie against Hapoel Tel Aviv for safety reasons

"A brave man dies once, a coward dies a million times."

Ken Bates referring to his players getting out of the Israel trip

"One day somebody will punch you."

Jose Mourinho on a Crystal Palace ball boy who spent too long giving the ball back

"If they don't touch me, I won't touch anyone. If they touch me, I'll be ready to hit back even harder."

Jose Mourinho on Sir Alex Ferguson and Arsene Wenger

"I can remember who was ready to whisper in an ear or two for their own ends. Now Vialli has found out that what goes around, comes around."

Ruud Gullit on Gianluca Vialli's dismissal

"Makelele is not a football player – Makelele is a slave. He's played the biggest game you can, the World Cup final, and now wants to retire. But the coach told us if he is not playing for France, he is not playing for Chelsea. We know the rules. You are a slave, you have no human rights."

Jose Mourinho is angry at France boss Raymond Domenech for taking Claude Makelele out of retirement

"Villa were like some two-bob team trying to get through on penalties."

Ken Bates on the 2000 FA Cup final win over the Villans

"The only club where her husband replaced me was at Inter Milan, where in six months he destroyed the best team in Europe at the time. And for her also to think about me and to speak about me, I think the lady needs to occupy her time, and if she takes care of her husband's diet she will have less time to speak about me."

Jose Mourinho on Rafael Benitez

"Take Ruud Gullit, I never liked his arrogance, in fact I never liked him. But while he was delivering the goods there was no problem. When he lost the plot, he had to go."

Ken Bates

"When others speak, maybe I don't take it on the chin. When players have not had a career, played at a really bad level in their career… Robbie Savage being one…"

John Terry hits back at criticism from TV pundit Robbie Savage

"Three years without a Premiership title? I don't think I would still be in a job."

Jose Mourinho barbs at Rafa Benitez

"We see a lot of Ken Bates. He'll always have a laugh and a joke with you. At your expense, obviously."

Graeme Le Saux

"Ricardo Carvalho seems to have problems understanding things, maybe he should have an IQ test, or go to a mental hospital or something."

Jose Mourinho after Ricardo Carvalho was upset the manager didn't start him

"I am what I am!!! Winnerrr!!!! Hahahahahahah, 11 to me 0 for you!!!"

Ashley Cole aims his tweet at Arsenal after winning his 11th trophy since leaving

"If [Jose] Mourinho is Jesus, then I am certainly not one of his apostles."

Carlo Ancelotti is not a fan

"There was never a relationship to begin with between me and Glenn Hoddle but you could say it deteriorated in that last year. Even the tea lady would have got a game before me."
Robert Fleck

"[Michael] Ballack, [Petr] Cech and [Didier] Drogba became my enemies. Somehow, they have a direct line to [Roman] Abramovich."
Luiz Felipe Scolari

"I was unhappy with my medical staff. They were impulsive and naive."
Jose Mourinho on Dr Eva Carneiro and physio Jon Fearn attending to Eden Hazard

"Mr Roth has two ways out, apologise or it goes to court."
Jose Mourinho responds after being called the "enemy of football" by UEFA referees' boss Volker Roth. Mourinho had wrongly accused Barcelona coach Frank Rijkaard of visiting referee Anders Frisk at half-time

"Without being unkind, we wouldn't try to sign a 61-year-old."
Ken Bates on rumours Chelsea approached Sir Alex Ferguson to be manager

MOURINHO V WENGER

"[Arsene] Wenger complaining is normal because he always does. Normally he should be happy that Chelsea sold a player like Juan Mata, but this is a little bit his nature. I think what is not fair is that his team always has the best days to play."

Jose Mourinho hits back at claims from Arsene Wenger that Chelsea selling Mata to Man United was unfair

"I'm not surprised, I'm not surprised. [Me] charged? Charged? If it was me it would have been a stadium ban."

The manager responds to journalists when it's suggested Arsene Wenger could be charged for shoving him

"Am I afraid of failure? He is a specialist in failure. I'm not. So if one supposes he's right and I'm afraid of failure, it's because I don't fail many times. So maybe he's right. I'm not used to failing. But the reality is he's a specialist because, eight years without a piece of silverware, that's failure. If I do that in Chelsea, eight years, I leave and don't come back."

Jose Mourinho hits back at Arsene Wenger who claimed the Chelsea manager has a fear of failure

"At Stamford Bridge, we have a file of quotes from Mr Wenger about Chelsea Football Club in the last 12 months – it is not a file of five pages. It is a file of 120 pages."

Jose Mourinho would be happy to see Arsene Wenger in court

"It's not easy. If it was easy, you wouldn't lose 3-1 at home to Monaco [in the Champions League last 16]."

Jose Mourinho replies to Arsene Wenger's suggestion that "it is easy to defend" in Europe

"Wenger has a real problem with us and I think he is what you call in England a voyeur. He is someone who likes to watch other people. There are some guys who, when they are at home, have this big telescope to look into the homes of other people and see what is happening. Wenger must be one of them – it is a sickness. He speaks, speaks, speaks about Chelsea."

Jose Mourinho makes a strong accusation

"Unlike Arsenal, we sought success and tried to build it through a concept of the game using English players."

Jose Mourinho attacks Arsene Wenger's recruitment policy

"If you add up the amounts the clubs have spent in the last three or four years I think maybe you will find a surprise. Get a calculator. That is one of the easiest things to do. It leaves no space for speculation. If you want to be honest, objective and pragmatic, it is the easiest job for a manager or a journalist to do. They have bought a fantastic goalkeeper and that is a position which is very important in a team. If you put Ozil plus Sanchez, plus Chambers, plus Debuchy you will maybe find a surprise."

Jose Mourinho jabs Arsene Wenger for his levels of spending

"The English like statistics a lot. Do they know that Arsene Wenger has only 50 per cent of wins in the English league?"

Jose Mourinho even uses stats to have a dig at the Frenchman

"You know, they like to cry. That's tradition. But I prefer to say, and I was telling it to the fourth official, that English people – Frank Lampard, for example – would never provoke a situation like that."

Jose Mourinho accuses Arsene Wenger's Arsenal of having a "tradition of crying"

"Many great managers have never won the Champions League – a big example is not far from us."

Jose Mourinho has another pop at Arsene Wenger

CALL THE MANAGER

"This is nothing against Sir Alex whatsoever. After the game on Wednesday we were together in my office and we spoke and drank wine. Unfortunately it was a very bad bottle of wine and he was complaining, so when we go to Old Trafford for the second leg, on my birthday, I will take a beautiful bottle of Portuguese wine."

Jose Mourinho on Sir Alex Ferguson

"A player from Man City showed half of his ass for two seconds and it was a big nightmare. But this is a real nightmare."

Jose Mourinho compares Petr Cech's bad injury with Joey Barton showing his bum

"Everybody is crying that Chelsea keep winning and winning and winning, so I think that draw at Goodison Park makes everyone more happy."

Jose Mourinho on losing the team's 100 per cent league record at Everton

"I've never been to Scarborough and I might even like the place."

Claudio Ranieri on his FA Cup opponents

"How many people does it take to make a banner? One. And maybe two to hold it."

Rafa Benitez on a 'Rafa Out' banner displayed at his first game as interim boss

"As we say in Portugal, they brought the bus and they left the bus in front of the goal. I would have been frustrated if I had been a supporter who paid £50 to watch this game because Spurs came to defend. There was only one team looking to win, they only came not to concede – it's not fair for the football we played."

Jose Mourinho after a 0-0 draw against Tottenham Hotspur

"When I hear them say they can win the title, it makes me feel like laughing."

Jose Mourinho on Liverpool

"At the end of today's third round, players you've never heard of will be household names – like that fellow who scored for Sutton United against Coventry last season."

Bobby Campbell

"That was not a football score, it was a hockey score… in training I often play matches of three against three and when the score reaches 5-4, I send the players back to the dressing room, because they are not defending properly."

Jose Mourinho on Arsenal's 5-4 win over Tottenham

"He is a great manager, he is clever and used his power and his prestige. The referee should not allow it. I have a lot of respect for Ferguson. I call him boss because he is the manager's boss. Maybe when I become 60, the kids will call me the same."

Jose Mourinho on Sir Alex Ferguson

"I saw their players and manager go for a lap of honour after losing to us in their last home game. In Portugal if you do this, they throw bottles at you."

Jose Mourinho on Manchester United

"I have a title. Someone decided the title would be 'interim'. Why? Just in case? If they want to blame me for everything that is wrong and then they say, 'We will put interim just in case', fine, that is your decision. I don't agree, but it's your decision and now everybody has to take responsibility."

Rafa Benitez doesn't like his Chelsea title

"Arsenal didn't have one single chance, including the goal."

Avram Grant

"The only way to stop Henry? With a gun!"

Gianluca Vialli on Thierry Henry

"During the afternoon it rained only in this stadium – our kitman saw it. There must be a microclimate here. It was like a swimming pool."

Jose Mourinho before a game at Blackburn

"I think we won that game against Liverpool because we scored and they didn't."

Jose Mourinho

CAN YOU MANAGE?

"When I talk to the players, I speak first of all in English, then I say, 'Sorry, now I will speak in Spanish, or Italian'. Then on the touchline I speak another language so the other manager doesn't understand what I am saying!"

Claudio Ranieri

"I have top players and, I'm sorry, we have a top manager. Please don't call me arrogant, but I'm European champion and I think I'm a special one."

Jose Mourinho

"I, Tinkerman, will not change."

Claudio Ranieri

"If the club decide to sack me because of bad results that's part of the game. If it happens, I will be a millionaire and get another club a couple of months later."

Jose Mourinho

"If I had been the owner, Ancelotti would have stayed, but I am not."

Carlo Ancelotti

"I am the Happy One."

Jose Mourinho on returning to Chelsea in 2013

"I am a very happy man and every day I wake up with a smile because it is a thrill to go to work. I know one day I will be sacked. That is inevitable. But I won't cry – I'll just say I did my best and move on."

Ruud Gullit shortly before getting fired

"I am happy when our fans are happy, when our players are happy and our chairman is on the moon."

Claudio Ranieri

"After 15 years, I'm an overnight success."

Jose Mourinho

"Pressure? There is no pressure. Bird flu is pressure. No, you laugh, but I am being serious. I am more worried about the swan then I am about football."

Jose Mourinho

"I am more scared of bird flu than football. What is football compared with life? I have to buy some masks and stuff – maybe for my team as well."

Jose Mourinho after Chelsea's lead over United slipped to seven points

"I can't change now. I'm like Frank Sinatra –
I always do it my way. I told the players
everything I did in the Monaco game was wrong.
I changed things to win the match – but we lost
and I was thinking 'Oh f*ck Claudio, why, why?
Bad Tinkerman!'"
Claudio Ranieri

"I am not the Special One. I'm the Normal One.
But my wife says I am special. What am I like? I
am 180cm."
Avram Grant

"I could say, 'What has he ever won?' but I won't."
Jose Mourinho on replacing Claudio Ranieri

Can You Manage?

"I would rather play with 10 men than wait for a player who is late for the bus."
Jose Mourinho on his managerial philosophy

"In Italy when Chelsea win, it is 'Chelsea win' or 'Abramovich wins' or 'Gudjohnsen wins'. When Chelsea lose, it is 'Ranieri loses'. But that is normal."
Claudio Ranieri

"They have to enjoy playing for me and Chelsea, but they don't have to be in love with me."
Jose Mourinho on his Chelsea players

"I am a lovely man as long as everyone does what I say."

Claudio Ranieri on joining Chelsea

"Why have Chelsea suffered so much since I left? Because I left."

Jose Mourinho after Luiz Felipe Scolari was sacked by Chelsea

"I don't know if you know, but with the football kit today there are no pockets. Nobody can put their hands in their pockets."

Avram Grant

"After all that has happened this season – and that is a lot – I've reached the conclusion that I am a good loser."

Jose Mourinho after losing the title to United in the 2006/07 season

"He must really think I'm a great guy. He must think that, because otherwise He would not have given me so much. I have a great family. I work in a place where I've always dreamt of working. He has helped me out so much that He must have a very high opinion of me."

Jose Mourinho on God

"I think Mr Ranieri will kick a few backsides, but only in a most pleasant manner."

Ray Wilkins

"My bad qualities are that I don't care about my image and because of that, I don't care about the consequences of what I say and the consequences of what I do."

Jose Mourinho

"I don't buy a player for his entertainment, because then you're going to work in a circus."

Ruud Gullit

Can You Manage?

"If I wanted to have an easy job... I would
have stayed at Porto – beautiful blue chair, the
UEFA Champions League trophy, God, and
after God, me."

Jose Mourinho on his new challenge

"People say we cannot play, that we are a
group of clowns. This is not right."

**Jose Mourinho on Chelsea's start to
2005/06**

"Chelsea have suffered in the last two years and it's no coincidence that this decline happened after I left."

Jose Mourinho

"Seeing this side develop has been like planting a seed and watching it grow like a flower."

Eddie McCreadie – two years before the club were relegated to the second tier

"I couldn't smoke before the match, but afterwards, oh yes!"

Carlo Ancelotti after winning his first game as Chelsea boss against Hull City

"I would love an Aston Martin, but if you ask me £1m for an Aston Martin, I tell you, you are crazy because they cost £250,000."

Jose Mourinho says he won't pay over the odds for a defender

"We all want to play great music all the time, but if that is not possible, you have to hit as many right notes as you can."

Jose Mourinho admits Chelsea aren't playing at their best

"He's a crazy man."

Claudio Ranieri on himself

"I want to push the young players on my team to have a proper haircut, not the Rastafarian or the others they have."

Jose Mourinho on why he shaved his hair

WOMAN TROUBLE

"John Hollins was a mistake. He has a very strong wife. It might have been better if I had made her manager."

Ken Bates

"I've heard Batesy's a pearler because he kicks every ball. Poor Suzannah must have loads of bruises."

Dennis Wise on chairman Ken Bates watching games with his wife

"I didn't get into girls until I was 18 because of football."

Roberto Di Matteo

"I never got sent any knickers, but girls who would write to ask where I hung out in my spare time and whether I was courting."
Gary Stanley

"Damien is Damien. When I don't put him in the squad my mother, who's 84, asks, 'Why isn't Damien playing?' She kills me about it and that's true."
The mum of Claudio Ranieri has a favourite

"The girls like Lampsy. If I was that way, I'd see something in him."
John Terry on Frank Lampard

"If I was having a race with my mum and I was expected to beat her by 50 yards, I'd like to beat her by 60 yards. I love winning."

Frank Sinclair

"You should never go back in life. You don't see many people out with their ex-wives, do you?"

Ken Bates doesn't want Dennis Wise returning to the club

"We play every three days. How can I be a good husband if I don't make love before each game?"

Frank Leboeuf

"My wife's the boss. Things don't happen just like that but if she says to me, 'Honey, I want to go to Paris Saint-Germain,' then I will have to take that into consideration."
Eden Hazard

"It all depends on my wife. If I am at home, yes, I will see it. But maybe my wife would like to go somewhere. I would like to see it – I like to see football and it is a big game. But maybe I will have no permission."
Jose Mourinho is not sure if he's allowed to watch Arsenal v Man United

"My only technical adviser is my mother. When I told her that Damien had injured his shoulder again, she said, 'Oh no! Who should replace him?' I will call her before the game to ask."

Claudio Ranieri

"The cook prepares very good food. I prefer to stay here and eat rather than going to my house. But don't tell my wife."

Gianfranco Zola

MEDIA
CIRCUS

"You have to remember I have managed in Italy and it's much, much, worse. In this country, the journalists want to kill you some of the time. In Italy, all of the time."

Claudio Ranieri

"I know the media all love me. They must care about me because they're always asking me, if I'm going to stay or go."

Avram Grant before his last Chelsea game

"The press in England make from a little mosquito a big elephant."

Ruud Gullit

"I can tell you now, to stop you [journalists] from asking, that as long as he is not scoring, Shevchenko will play."
Jose Mourinho on Andriy Shevchenko's lack of goals

"I don't know if he will be captain next season... I joke.... I like to joke in press conferences."
New manager Carlo Ancelotti when asked about John Terry's future

"Hello my sharks, welcome to the funeral."
Claudio Ranieri greets the press before Chelsea's Champions League semi-final, second leg, against Monaco

"I said I wanted the same car as James Bond and the reporter got the wrong end of the stick and said I wanted to be James Bond!"

Joe Cole

"Would you phone the president of Ghana?"

Jose Mourinho when asked by a Ghanaian journalist if he ever called owner Roman Abramovich to see how he was

"I never speak, according to the newspapers. I just storm and blast."

Ken Bates

"Facing the press is not easy, but because you have to go, you have to try to take a lot of positive things for yourself from these face-to-face meetings."
Jose Mourinho

"I have been let down so often, read so much that wasn't remotely true, that I now find it difficult to trust anyone who shows up with a notebook and pen."
John Hollins

"The thing I don't enjoy [about English football] is the way the media talk about us. I feel as if the knives are being aimed in our direction, while the flowers are in another."

Jose Mourinho

"I must say thank you to the media, because you do a great job now. Before you kill me! That crazy man! I give you a good espresso. A small one. I am Scottish man!"

Claudio Ranieri on rumours his tenure was coming to an end

"You won't see me in 20 or 30 years' time, sitting and slagging off an England performance. Shoot me if you do."
Frank Lampard on the TV pundits who slammed the team at the 2006 World Cup

"When a dog three-months-old is the front page of a newspaper in this country, you cannot believe the things you read."
Jose Mourinho after he was arrested for arguing with police over his dog

"I'm off to my 300-acre farm. You lot can bugger off to your council houses."

Ken Bates to the press after the Blues were relegated

"I have nothing, nothing to say. Nothing, nothing to say. Nothing to say, I have nothing to say. Nothing to say, I am so sorry, I have nothing to say."

Jose Mourinho when asked four separate questions from BT Sport's Des Kelly after a 3-1 loss against Liverpool

"When I go to the press conference before the game, in my mind the game has already started."
Jose Mourinho

"And when I go to the press conference after the game, the game has not finished yet."
Jose Mourinho

"The 'Save Ranieri' campaign in the Evening Standard is flattering save for one thing.
They can't run a picture of me in my glasses.
Gladiators don't wear glasses in the Colosseum."
Claudio Ranieri

"The English press, if you understand their philosophy, it was very funny to play their game. Salt and pepper every day."

Jose Mourinho

BOARDROOM BANTER

"One beautiful day, a radiant day, Mr Abramovich introduced himself to me and said I should put a shopping list together."
Claudio Ranieri

"We passed like ships in the night. He was a huge yacht, I was a little rowing boat."
Graeme Le Saux on leaving Chelsea as Roman Abramovich came in

"I parted on good terms with Luca Vialli. As he left the room and I led him to the door, we departed with the usual Italian formalities of a bear hug and a kiss."
Ken Bates

"He's a real Chelsea fan. When we lose a difficult match, he's sulking and there are tears in his eyes."
Bruce Buck, Chelsea chairman, on Roman Abramovich

"If Roman Abramovich helped me out in training, we would be bottom of the league and if I had to work in his world of big business, we would be bankrupt!"
Jose Mourinho

"I'm not star-struck around players. How could I be? I'm the biggest star here."
Ken Bates

"The winner of the Premier League will come from a select bunch of one."

Peter Kenyon, Chelsea chief executive

"The reason why we haven't signed any English players is that there aren't enough good ones about, as the European Championship showed."

Ken Bates

"[Roman] Abramovich knows nothing about football. I already have his sword sticking in me... Even if I win the European Cup, I'll be sacked."

Claudio Ranieri

"We had to make a change. There is no easy way to do it. Do you go for a shot in the head or a death from a thousand cuts?"

Ken Bates on sacking Gianluca Vialli

"Mr Abramovich is almost like one of the lads, if a billionaire can be."

John Terry

"Hump it, bump it, whack. That may be a recipe for a good sex life, but it won't win us the World Cup."

Ken Bates on the England team

"I had one agent phoning up saying, 'I have the honour of representing one of the world's greatest players, he needs no introduction.' I said, 'You're right, I don't want to meet him'."
Ken Bates

"I don't seek publicity, it seeks me."
Ken Bates

Printed in Great Britain
by Amazon

33016383R00078